21st Century Junior Library

T002293

INFOGRAPHICS: EVERY SECOND COUNTS

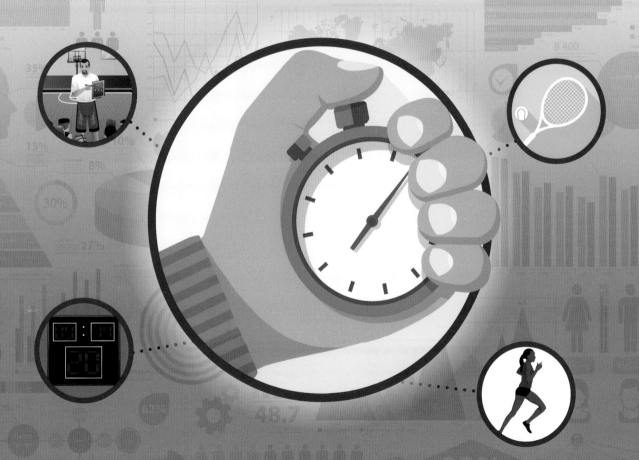

Sports-Graphics Jr.

Kristy Stark

Published in the United States of America by:

CHERRY LAKE PRESS
2395 South Huron Parkway, Suite 200, Ann Arbor, Michigan 48104
www.cherrylakepress.com

Reading Adviser: Beth Walker Gambro, MS, Ed., Reading Consultant, Yorkville, IL

Photo Credits: © hvostik/Shutterstock, © artisticco/Getty Images, © stevezmina1/Getty Images, © msan10/Getty Images, © FARBAI/ Getty Images, cover; © Art Alex/Shutterstock, 4; © kupritz/Getty Images, 7; © nikiteev_konstantin/Shutterstock, 12; © Aşkın Dursun KAMBEROĞLU/Getty Images, © rambo182/Getty Images, © Jessica Orozco, © bounward / Getty Images, © lushik/Getty Images, © pop_ jop/Getty Images, 14; © GoodStudio/Shutterstock, 16; © biolalabet/Shutterstock, 19

Cherry Lake Press is an imprint of Cherry Lake Publishing Group.

Library of Congress Cataloging-in-Publication Data has been filed and is available at catalog.loc.gov.

Cherry Lake Publishing Group would like to acknowledge the work of the Partnership for 21st Century Learning, a Network of Battelle for Kids. Please visit Battelle for Kids online for more information.

Printed in the United States of America

Note from publisher: Websites change regularly, and their future contents are outside of our control. Supervise children when conducting any recommended online searches for extended learning opportunities.

ABOUT THE AUTHOR

Kristy Stark writes books about a variety of topics, from sports to biographies to science topics. When she is not busy writing, she enjoys reading, camping, lounging at the beach, and doing just about anything outdoors. Most of all, she loves to spend time with her husband, daughter, son, and two lazy cats at their home in Southern California.

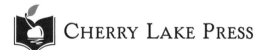

CHERRY LAKE PRESS

CONTENTS

A Matter of Seconds 4

How Sports Are Timed 5

Speed and Velocity 9

Training for Victory 13

Breaking Records 17

Activity 22

Find Out More 23

Glossary 24

Index 24

A MATTER OF SECONDS

The seconds on the clock tick down . . . 3 . . . 2 . . . 1. She shoots the ball. She scores just before the clock hits zero. The fans go wild!

No matter the sport, every second counts. So much can happen in a few seconds. The **outcome** of the game can even change in fractions of a second.

HOW SPORTS ARE TIMED

Every sport has its own way of dividing the game or match. Each part has a certain amount of time. A football game is divided into four quarters. In the National Football League (NFL), each quarter is 15 minutes. High school football games typically have 12-minute quarters.

Soccer games are divided into halves. Hockey games are played in three periods.

QUARTERS, HALVES, AND PERIODS IN SPORTS

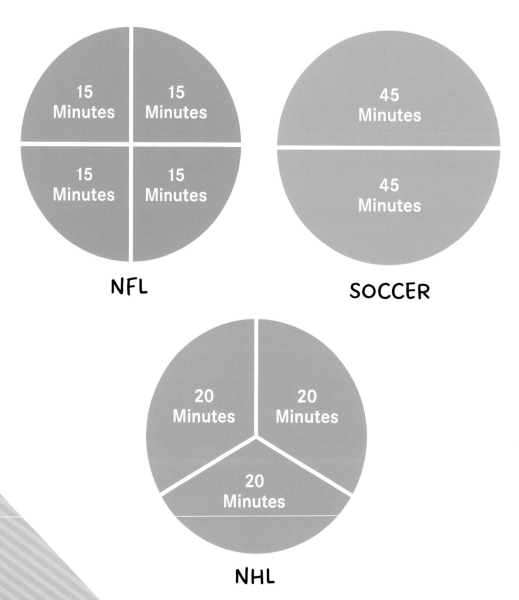

NFL

| 15 Minutes | 15 Minutes |
| 15 Minutes | 15 Minutes |

SOCCER

45 Minutes / 45 Minutes

NHL

20 Minutes / 20 Minutes / 20 Minutes

2022, Rookie Road; 2022, FloHockey; 2022, Sports Illustrated

AVERAGE NFL TV BROADCAST

An NFL game clocks 60 minutes of playing time. The games last much longer. The length of the game depends on television **coverage.** Commercial breaks add time.

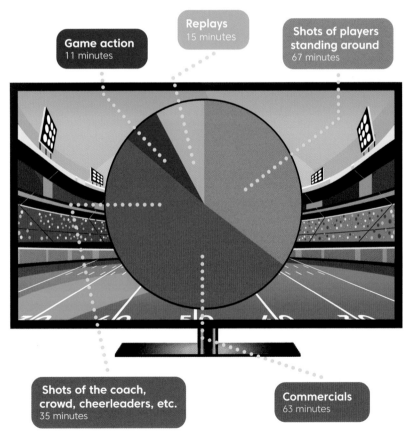

Game action
11 minutes

Replays
15 minutes

Shots of players standing around
67 minutes

Shots of the coach, crowd, cheerleaders, etc.
35 minutes

Commercials
63 minutes

2022, Daily Snark

CLOCKS IN SPORTS

In addition to game clocks, many sports have **play clocks** and **shot clocks.** These show how long a player has to make a play or start an action.

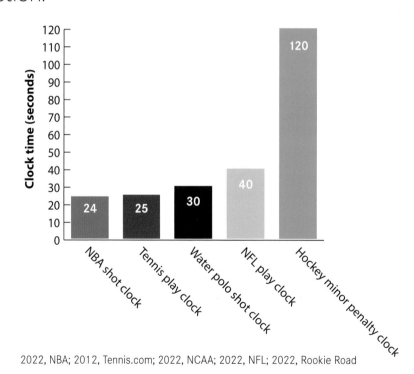

2022, NBA; 2012, Tennis.com; 2022, NCAA; 2022, NFL; 2022, Rookie Road

SPEED AND VELOCITY

While the clock runs, athletes want to make the most of their time. They can do a lot during that time. They have to move, hit, and run as fast as they can.

Speed plays a huge role in sports. Speed is the rate of time at which an object or body moves along a path. From running to pitching to swimming, the faster the better.

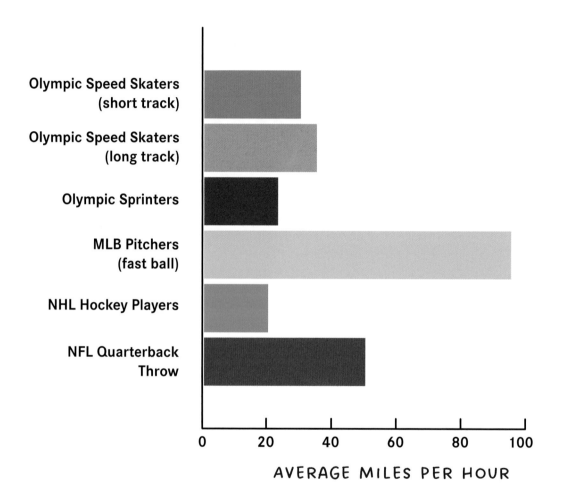

ATHLETES' AVERAGE SPEEDS

Olympic Speed Skaters (short track)

Olympic Speed Skaters (long track)

Olympic Sprinters

MLB Pitchers (fast ball)

NHL Hockey Players

NFL Quarterback Throw

AVERAGE MILES PER HOUR

0   20   40   60   80   100

2022, NBC Bay Area; 2021, New York Times; 2022, The Champlair.
com; 2011, Wonderopolis.org; 2020, Reference.com

Athletes and coaches also track **velocity.** This is the rate and direction of an object's movement. Think of a baseball pitcher. The velocity of a pitch is the maximum speed of a pitch from its release until it crosses home plate. The number of 100 miles (161 kilometers) per hour pitches in the MLB is growing fast.

NUMBER OF 100+ MILES (161+ KM) PER HOUR PITCHES

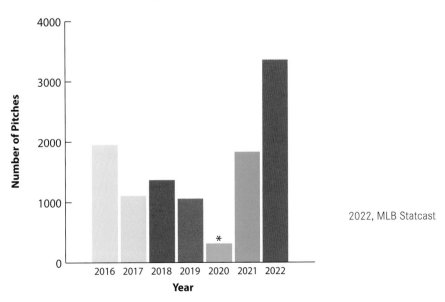

2022, MLB Statcast

*The 2020 season was shortened because of the COVID-19 pandemic.

AVERAGE SPEEDS BY EVENT

Sprinters run faster than long distance runners.

A sprinter needs to keep their pace for seconds.

A long distance runner keeps their pace for hours.

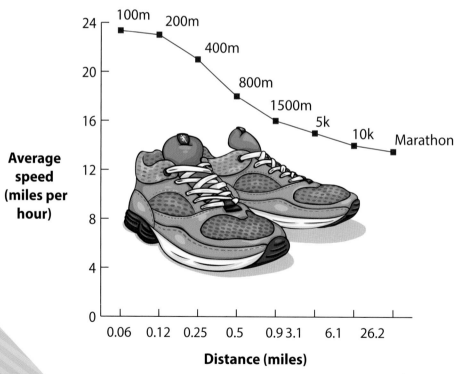

2021, New York Times

TRAINING FOR VICTORY

Athletes do whatever they can to perform their best. The fastest runner wins the race. The speed skater with the fastest time beats her **opponents.** The hockey player who can make the quickest shot is more likely to score. So athletes work hard to get faster. Players train harder. They need to be able to **shave** off time to win.

AN ATHLETE'S BRAIN

System 1: Seconds to Act	System 2: Hours to Train
Fast	Slow
Unconscious	Conscious
Automatic	Effortful
Everyday Decisions	Complex Decisions
Error Prone	Reliable

2017, Ball State University Sports Link

Football coaches need quarterbacks who can run fast. They need wide receivers who are fast. A tenth of a second can make a difference.

Coaches look to the **NFL Combine.** There, they **recruit** players. The players run a 40-yard dash. These results help coaches find the fastest players.

NFL COMBINE 2022

Player	Position	School	40-Yard Dash (seconds)
Kalon Barnes	CB	Baylor	4.23
Tariq Woolen	CB	Texas-San Antonio	4.26
Tyquan Thornton	WR	Baylor	4.28
Velus Jones Jr.	WR	Tennessee	4.31
Calvin Austin III	WR	Memphis	4.32

2022, NFL

ALTITUDE AFFECTS BASEBALL

Training plays a big role in an athlete's performance. But there are other factors that a player cannot control. **Elevation** can play a role in how far a baseball travels.

If the same ball was thrown at both parks, it would travel at different speeds.

SEATTLE MARINERS, 10 feet (3.04 meters) elevation
A pitcher throws a fastball.

It travels at 100 miles (161 km) per hour.

It takes 0.413 seconds **to reach the plate.**

COLORADO ROCKIES, 5200 feet (1585 m) elevation
A pitcher throws the same fastball.

It travels at 102 miles (164 km) per hour.

It takes 0.405 seconds **to reach the plate.**

The Rockies' ball travels 2 percent faster.

2021, CU Boulder Today; 2022, Maplogs; 2011, The Physics of Baseball; 2020, Baseball Cloud Blog

BREAKING RECORDS

A game can come down to the last seconds. A lot can happen with only a few seconds left on the game clock.

Fractions of a second can break a world record time. It can come down to tenths or hundredths of a second! How fast is that? Think of it this way: The average human eye blinks in about a tenth of a second. So the short time it takes to blink could mean the difference between first and second place.

100-METER DASH TIMES (MEN)

	Year	Time & Athlete	Rank	
	1936	10.2 seconds; Jesse Owens	9	
	1956	10.1 seconds; Ira Murchison	8	
	1968	9.95 seconds; Jim Hines	7	
	1972	9.9 seconds; Eddie Hart	6	
	1978	9.87 seconds; William Snoddy	5	
	1988	9.78 seconds; Carl Lewis	4	
	1996	9.69 seconds; Obadele Thompson	3	
	2008	9.68 seconds; Tyson Gay	2	
	2009	9.58 seconds; Usain Bolt	1	

2021, World Athletics

LONGEST OVERTIME FOOTBALL GAMES

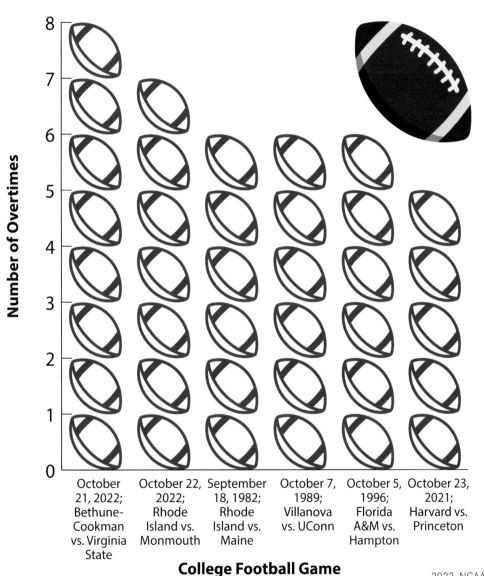

Number of Overtimes (y-axis: 0 to 8)

College Football Game (x-axis)

Game	Number of Overtimes
October 21, 2022; Bethune-Cookman vs. Virginia State	8
October 22, 2022; Rhode Island vs. Monmouth	7
September 18, 1982; Rhode Island vs. Maine	6
October 7, 1989; Villanova vs. UConn	6
October 5, 1996; Florida A&M vs. Hampton	6
October 23, 2021; Harvard vs. Princeton	5

SHORTEST TENNIS MATCHES ON RECORD

On average, a **professional** tennis match lasts anywhere from about 90 minutes to over 2 hours. But some players have broken records by how quickly they were able to defeat their opponents.

Helen Wills defeated Joan Fry in 24 minutes. (1927)

Margaret Court defeated Darlene Hard in 24 minutes. (1963)

Jarkko Nieminen defeated Bernard Tomic in 28 minutes. (2014)

2021, Tennis Predict

Jack Harper defeated J. Sandiford in 18 minutes. (1946)

William Renshaw defeated John Hartley in 36 minutes. (1881)

Steffi Graf defeated Natasha Zvereva in 34 minutes. (1988)

Francisco Clavet defeated Jiang Shan in 25 minutes. (2001)

ACTIVITY

Time Yourself!

You know that athletes train to improve their skills and to increase their speed. Pick an activity that you want to improve. For example, you can time how long it takes you to run a mile or the time it takes to do 50 sit-ups.

Materials Needed

- Stopwatch or timer
- Paper
- Writing utensil

Time yourself doing the same activity over the course of 5 days. Record your time each day on the table below. After 5 days, graph your results.

Day	Time
1	
2	
3	
4	
5	

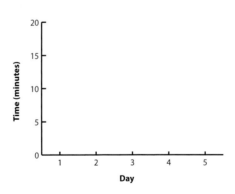

1. Did your time increase or decrease over the 5 days?
2. What did you do to improve your time?
3. Estimate the difference between your fastest time and your slowest time.

FIND OUT MORE

Books

Buckley, James Jr. *It's a Numbers Game! Baseball: The Math Behind the Perfect Pitch, the Game-Winning Grand Slam, and So Much More!* Washington, DC: National Geographic Kids, 2021.

Storden, Thom. *Big-Time Football Records.* North Mankato, MN: Capstone Press, 2021.

Online Resources to Explore with an Adult

Kiddle: Tennis Facts for Kids

National Geographic Kids: 10 Facts About the Olympics!

Bibliography

"The Longest Overtime Games in FCS College Football History." NCAA.com. October 2022.

"How Speed and Distance Dictate How Olympians Run." New York Times. July 2021.

"2022 Combine Results." NFL.com. March 2022.

"How Long Is Soccer Halftime at the World Cup?" Sports Illustrated. November 2022.

World Athletics. Records by Event. February 2021.

GLOSSARY

coverage (KUH-ver-uhj) the reporting of an event in the media

elevation (eh-luh-VAY-shun) the height of a place

NFL Combine (EN-EF-EL KAHM-bine) an annual event where coaches and scouts watch potential players complete physical and mental tests

opponents (uh-POH-nuhnts) people or teams who are competing against each other

outcome (OWT-kuhm) the result of an activity or process

play clocks (PLAY KLAHKS) clocks that count down how long teams or players have to make an action

professional (pruh-FEH-shuh-nuhl) having to do with a job that requires special skills, training, or experience

recruit (ruh-KROOT) to find the right people for the job or team

shave (SHAYV) to reduce something by taking away a small amount

shot clocks (SHAHT KLAHKS) clocks that count down how long teams or players have to try to score

sprinters (SPRIN-turs) runners who race over a short distance at a very fast speed

velocity (vuh-LAH-suh-tee) how quickly an object is moving

INDEX

40-yard dash, 15

brain, 14

coaches, 7, 11, 15
Colorado Rockies, 16

Major League Baseball (MLB), 10–11

National Basketball Association (NBA), 8
National Football League (NFL), 5–8, 10, 15
National Hockey League (NHL), 6, 10

runners, 12–13

Seattle Mariners, 16

tennis, 8, 20
timeout, 8